HELEN CHEN

Peking Cuisine

HELEN CHEN

Peking Cuisine

Photography by Simon Wheeler

WEIDENFELD & NICOLSON

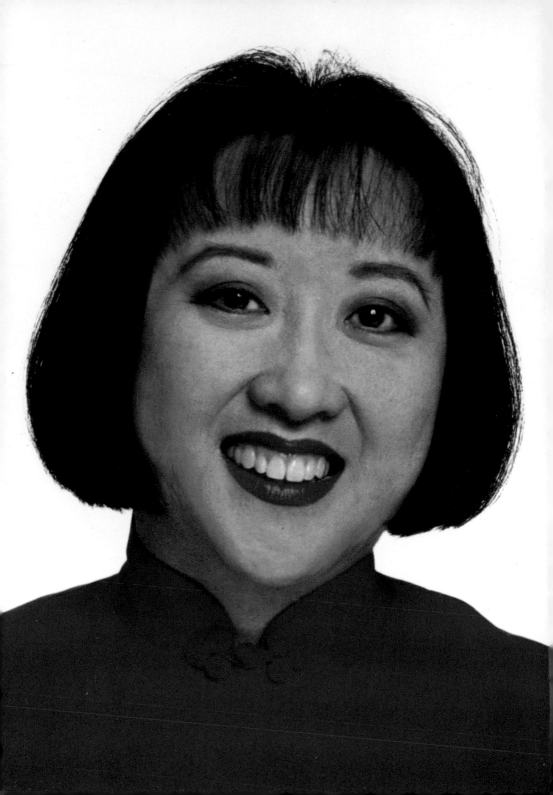

Helen Chen

Helen Chen was born in Shanghai, China, and learned to cook traditional Shanghai and Peking dishes from her mother, Joyce Chen, the grande dame of Chinese cuisine in the United States. A respected culinary expert in her own right, Helen is the author of several cookbooks, including *Helen Chen's Chinese Home Cooking* (1994, Hearst Books). She is also a director of Joyce Chen, Inc, a speciality cookware company. Helen travels regularly to China and the Far East to search for and develop new kitchen products and recipes and to visit her extended family, which numbers more than 40 first cousins.

Contents

Cooking

is an art – an unselfish art

which is to be

enjoyed and shared

with others.

JOYCE CHEN
1917–1994

Introduction

My mother was from Peking, China and many of my favourite childhood dishes are from this region. I love the variety, rich flavours and history that Peking cuisine infuses into every dish.

Moo shi pork and hot and sour soup are Peking classics that incorporate the exotic flavours and textures of tiger lily buds and black tree fungus. The area around Peking is the only part of China where there are lamb dishes, a legacy of the Mongols, who conquered northern China in the 13th century. Wheat, rather than rice, is the traditional crop of the region, so wheat is favoured, and noodles and pancakes are de rigueur in Peking. Peking meat sauce noodles and homestyle spring onion pancakes are Peking street food at its best – and so easy to make at home!

The city of Peking is now more often referred to as Beijing, but it is one of those place names that is recognizable, and somehow more familiar, in its older form. China adopted the new system of romanizing words (known as 'pinyin', or piece-together-sound) after the founding of the People's Republic of China in 1949, when the Mandarin dialect became the national language, uniting all the provinces in a common tongue.

Enjoy your introduction to Peking cuisine. I hope you'll come back for more.

Helen Chen

PEKING HOT AND SOUR SOUP

SERVES 4

15 g/½ oz (about 40 pieces)
  dried golden needles, soaked
  and drained (page 34)
3–4 dried wood ears, soaked and
  drained (page 36)
85 g/3 oz lean pork, shredded
1 teaspoon rice wine or dry
  sherry
3 tablespoons cornflour
1 litre/1¾ pints chicken stock
1 tablespoon light soy sauce
85 g/3 oz soft bean curd
  (tofu), shredded
1 egg, beaten
2 tablespoons cider vinegar
¼ teaspoon ground white pepper
1½ teaspoons sesame seed oil
½ teaspoon salt, or to taste
1 spring onion, very thinly sliced

Trim off the tough ends of the golden needles and any tough parts of the wood ears. Cut the golden needles in half and coarsely chop the wood ears. Set aside.

Put the pork in a small bowl with the rice wine and 1 teaspoon of the cornflour. Set aside. Dissolve the remaining cornflour in 125 ml/4 fl oz cold water and set aside.

Put the chicken stock and soy sauce in a saucepan and bring to the boil. When the stock is boiling, stir in the pork and cook until it separates, about 30 seconds. Then stir in the golden needles and wood ears. Allow the stock to come back to the boil and cook for 1 minute. Add the bean curd and, as soon as the stock comes back to the boil, stir the cornflour mixture and add it to the soup, stirring constantly until the soup thickens.

Still stirring constantly, pour the beaten egg into the hot soup in a steady stream. Remove from the heat and immediately stir in the vinegar, pepper and sesame seed oil. Add salt to taste and garnish with spring onion. Serve hot.

This hearty soup makes a perfect cold-weather snack or light lunch when served with triangles of Homestyle spring onion pancakes (page 12). Alternatively, serve as the soup course in a multi-course meal.

HOMESTYLE SPRING ONION PANCAKES

SERVES 4 – 8

2 eggs, beaten

175 g/6 oz flour

4 spring onions (green and white
    parts), thinly sliced

2 rashers of bacon,
    finely chopped

250 ml/8 fl oz chicken stock

½ teaspoon salt

3 tablespoons vegetable oil

In a bowl, mix together the eggs, flour, spring onions, bacon, stock and salt to make a thin batter.

Heat 2 teaspoons of the oil in a hot frying pan (25 cm/ 10 inches in diameter) over medium heat. Tip the pan so that the oil spreads across the bottom of the pan, then pour in a quarter of the batter and spread, using a spatula, until it covers the bottom of the pan.

Cook until the edges are slightly brown, then turn the pancake over and lightly brown the other side. Repeat with the remaining oil and batter, to make four pancakes. Cut into wedges and serve hot.

Cut the cooked pancakes into triangles (and, if you like, roll them up and secure with a cocktail stick) for a delicious hors d'oeuvre. My mother used to make these for us as a nutritious after-school snack.

CUCUMBER AND CHICKEN SHREDS
in spicy peanut sauce

SERVES 4 AS PART OF
A MULTI-COURSE MEAL

2 cucumbers (about 450 g/1 lb)
4 tablespoons smooth peanut
    butter
4 tablespoons chicken stock
1 tablespoon light soy sauce
¼ teaspoon Szechuan
    peppercorns, toasted and
    ground
1 tablespoon sesame seed oil
1 teaspoon dried chilli flakes, or
    to taste
50 g/2 oz cooked chicken,
    shredded
salt
25 g/1 oz dry-roasted unsalted
    peanuts, coarsely chopped

Partially peel the cucumbers, leaving alternate strips of green skin for colour and texture. Cut the cucumbers in half lengthways, then scoop out and discard the seeds. Cut the cucumbers on the diagonal into thin slices.

In a small bowl, combine the peanut butter, stock, soy sauce, Szechuan peppercorns, sesame seed oil and chilli flakes. Mix to a smooth, thin paste.

When ready to serve, toss the cucumber slices and shredded chicken together with the peanut dressing and add salt to taste. Sprinkle with the chopped peanuts.

Perfect by itself as a light lunch salad, with slices of crusty bread.

MOO SHI PORK

**SERVES 3 – 4, OR 5 – 6 AS PART OF
A MULTI-COURSE MEAL**

150 g/5 oz lean pork, shredded
2 teaspoons rice wine or
    dry sherry
2 tablespoons light soy sauce
1 teaspoon cornflour
25 g/1 oz dried golden needles,
    soaked and drained (page 34)
3–4 dried wood ears, soaked
    and drained (page 36)
3 tablespoons vegetable oil
4 eggs, beaten
1 slice of fresh ginger
2 spring onions (green and white
    parts), thinly sliced
150 g/5 oz drained bamboo
    shoots, shredded
½ teaspoon salt

To serve
8–10 Mandarin pancakes
    (page 35), steamed
hoisin sauce

Mix the pork with the rice wine, soy sauce and cornflour. Set aside.

Trim off the tough ends of the golden needles and any tough parts of the wood ears. Cut the golden needles in half and coarsely chop the wood ears. Set aside.

Heat 2 tablespoons of the oil in a wok over medium-high heat. When the oil is hot, add the eggs and cook for about 2 minutes, stirring constantly, until scrambled finely. Remove and set aside.

Pour the remaining oil into the wok over high heat. Add the ginger and stir a few times until it sizzles. Stir the pork mixture and add it to the wok, stirring a few times to separate the shreds, then add the spring onions, bamboo shoots, wood ears, golden needles and salt. Continue stirring over high heat until the vegetables are heated through and the pork is thoroughly cooked, about 2–3 minutes. Return the eggs to the wok and mix well. Serve hot, with steamed pancakes and hoisin sauce.

This classic Peking dish is a fabulous appetizer or a meal in itself. Instead of the pancakes, it could be served with steamed or boiled rice.

PRAWNS WITH MANGETOUT

**SERVES 3 – 4, OR 5 – 6 AS PART OF
A MULTI-COURSE MEAL**

450 g/1 lb large uncooked
    prawns, shelled and deveined
¼ teaspoon grated fresh ginger
1 teaspoon rice wine or dry
    sherry
1 teaspoon cornflour
½ teaspoon salt
3 tablespoons vegetable oil
125 g/4 oz mangetout, ends
    snapped and strings removed

Rinse the prawns in cold water, drain and place in a bowl. Stir in the ginger, rice wine, cornflour and salt and mix well. Set aside.

Heat 1 tablespoon of the oil in a wok over medium-high heat. When the oil is hot, but not smoking, add the mangetout and stir until they turn a darker green, about 1 minute. Remove the mangetout and spread out on a plate.

Pour the remaining oil into the same wok over high heat. Stir the prawn mixture and add to the wok. Stir constantly for about 1 minute, or until the prawns turn pink and opaque. Return the mangetout to the wok and stir together over high heat for about 30 seconds. Transfer to a serving dish and serve immediately.

As part of a multi-course meal with steamed rice, this light dish pairs nicely with the dark sauces of either Lamb with spring onions (page 28) or Chicken with walnuts (page 24).

BEAN CURD AND CRABMEAT

**SERVES 3 – 4, OR 5 – 6 AS PART OF
A MULTI-COURSE MEAL**

175 g/6 oz canned crabmeat,
    drained
1 teaspoon rice wine or dry
    sherry
450 g/1 lb firm bean curd (tofu)
3 tablespoons vegetable oil
2 slices of fresh ginger
250 ml/8 fl oz chicken stock
2 tablespoons cornflour
    dissolved in 4 tablespoons
    chicken stock
1 egg white, lightly beaten
salt
2 spring onions, thinly sliced

Place the crabmeat in a small bowl and mix in the rice wine. Set aside. Drain the bean curd and cut into 2.5 cm/1 inch cubes. Set aside.

Heat the oil in a wok over medium–high heat. Add the ginger and stir until fragrant. Add the crabmeat and stock, stirring gently. Reduce the heat to medium–low, add the bean curd and simmer for about 4 minutes.

Raise the heat to high and when the mixture comes to a boil, stir in the cornflour mixture. Continue stirring until the mixture thickens and returns to the boil, then stir in the egg white, to form filmy clouds. Remove the wok from the heat and taste, adding salt if necessary. Pour into a deep serving dish and sprinkle with spring onions. Serve immediately.

Low-fat and meat-free, this is excellent as a light dish served with steamed rice. As part of a multi-course meal, serve with heartier fare such as Chicken with walnuts (page 24) or Beef with green and red peppers (page 30).

STIR-FRIED SPINACH

SERVES 4

450 g/1 lb fresh spinach
2 tablespoons vegetable oil
2 garlic cloves, lightly crushed
½ teaspoon salt
1 teaspoon sugar

Separate the spinach into leaves – do not remove the stalks – and wash thoroughly in several changes of cold water. Drain well.

Heat the oil in a wok over high heat. When the oil is hot, add the garlic and salt. Stir a few times until fragrant, then add the well-drained spinach. Stir constantly until the spinach begins to wilt, then add the sugar and continue stirring until the spinach is well wilted, about 1–2 minutes. Spread on a shallow platter and serve immediately.

Quick, easy and nutritious, this makes a great vegetable dish in a multi-course Chinese dinner, but can equally well be served as a side dish with Western food. It's excellent with fish.

Chicken with walnuts

**SERVES 3 – 4, OR 5 – 6 AS PART OF
A MULTI-COURSE MEAL**

450 g/1 lb skinless, boneless
    chicken breast, cut into
    2 cm/¾ inch cubes
2 teaspoons cornflour
2 teaspoons rice wine or dry
    sherry
½ teaspoon grated fresh ginger
2 tablespoons hoisin sauce
1 teaspoon sugar
2 tablespoons dark soy sauce
4 tablespoons vegetable oil
2 garlic cloves, lightly crushed
85 g/3 oz shelled walnut halves,
    toasted
1 teaspoon sesame seed oil

Place the chicken in a bowl and add the cornflour, rice wine and ginger. Mix well and set aside.

In a small bowl, mix the hoisin sauce, sugar, soy sauce and 2 tablespoons water. Stir until smooth and set aside.

Heat the oil and garlic in a wok over high heat until the oil is hot and the garlic sizzles. Stir the chicken mixture again and add it to the wok. Stir for 1–2 minutes, until the chicken is almost done. Remove the garlic if desired.

Reduce the heat to medium and stir in the sauce mixture. Continue stirring until well blended, then add the walnuts and sesame seed oil. Give a few big stirs with a spatula, then serve immediately.

The rich and unusual flavours make this ideal as the main course of a Western-style dinner, accompanied by rice and a dish of steamed or stir-fried vegetables. Instead of the walnuts, you could use oven-roasted unsalted cashew nuts.

PEKING MEAT SAUCE NOODLES

SERVES 6

(MAKES 600 ML/1 PINT SAUCE)

225 g/8 oz minced pork

2 teaspoons rice wine or dry
   sherry

2 teaspoons cornflour

2 tablespoons hoisin sauce

1 tablespoon dark soy sauce

1 tablespoon sugar

7 tablespoons bean paste or
   Japanese miso

250 ml/8 fl oz water

1 tablespoon vegetable oil

2 garlic cloves, finely chopped

1 onion, finely chopped

2 spring onions (green and white
   parts), thinly sliced

450 g/1 lb egg noodles or thin
   spaghetti

To garnish

6–8 radishes, shredded

1 cucumber, peeled, seeded
   and shredded

200 g/7 oz bean sprouts,
   parboiled for 15 seconds and
   drained

325 g/12 oz spinach, parboiled
   for 15 seconds, squeezed dry
   and finely chopped

Mix the pork with the rice wine and cornflour. Set aside. In another bowl, mix the hoisin sauce, soy sauce, sugar, bean paste and water. Set aside.

Heat the oil in a wok over high heat. When the oil is hot, add the pork mixture and stir until the meat becomes opaque and separates, about 2 minutes. Add the garlic and onion and continue stirring for another minute. Then add the spring onions and stir for another minute, until the spring onions are wilted.

Add the bean paste mixture and stir thoroughly into the meat; the sauce will be thin. Reduce the heat to low and simmer for 3–4 minutes.

Bring 5 litres/9 pints of water to a boil in a large saucepan. Add the noodles or spaghetti and boil until it is a little more tender than al dente. Drain and rinse in hot water. Divide the noodles between six individual bowls. Transfer the meat sauce to a serving bowl and place on the table. Set the vegetable garnishes, each in their own bowls, on the table. Allow your guests to add their own sauce and garnishes.

The vegetable garnishes provide colour and texture to make this a complete meal for a satisfying lunch or simple dinner. As additional or alternative garnishes, you could serve shredded crisp lettuce, or blanched and shredded mangetout.

LAMB WITH SPRING ONIONS

**SERVES 3–4, OR 5–6 AS PART OF
A MULTI-COURSE MEAL**

450 g/1 lb boneless loin of lamb
1 tablespoon cornflour
1 tablespoon rice wine or dry
  sherry
2 tablespoons dark soy sauce
2 tablespoons hoisin sauce
1 teaspoon sugar
3 tablespoons vegetable oil
1 slice of fresh ginger
2 garlic cloves, crushed
6 spring onions (green and white
  parts), cut into 5 cm/2 inch
  pieces
1 teaspoon sesame seed oil

Cut the lamb against the grain into 5 cm/2 inch slices, 3 mm/⅛ inch thick. Place the lamb in a bowl, add the cornflour, rice wine, soy sauce, hoisin sauce and sugar and mix well. Set aside.

Heat the oil in a wok over medium-high heat. Add the ginger and garlic and stir a few times until fragrant. Stir the lamb mixture and add to the wok, stirring constantly for about 1 minute or until the lamb changes colour and separates.

Stir in 3 tablespoons water and add the spring onions, stirring constantly for 1–2 minutes, until the spring onions are wilted and the lamb is fully cooked. Add the sesame seed oil and stir a few times, then serve immediately.

The Chinese believe lamb has warming properties, so this is an excellent dish to serve in the cold winter months, with rice or noodles. Whole tangerines or mango halves would make a light and refreshing dessert.

BEEF WITH GREEN AND RED PEPPERS

**SERVES 3 – 4, OR 5 – 6 AS PART OF
A MULTI-COURSE MEAL**

450 g/1 lb flank steak
2 tablespoons dark soy sauce
1 teaspoon rice wine or dry
    sherry
1 teaspoon cornflour
1 teaspoon sugar
3 tablespoons vegetable oil
1 red pepper, seeded, cored and
    cut into 5 x 1 cm/2 x ½ inch
    strips
1 green pepper, seeded, cored
    and cut into 5 x 1 cm/2 x
    ½ inch strips
2 slices of fresh ginger
2 garlic cloves, crushed
salt

Trim the fat from the meat and cut along the grain into long strips, about 5 cm/2 inches wide. Then slice the strips across the grain into thin slices, about 3 mm/ ⅛ inch. Place the beef in a bowl, add the soy sauce, rice wine, cornflour and sugar and mix well. Set aside.

Heat 1 tablespoon of the oil in a wok over medium-high heat until hot. Add the peppers and stir for 1 minute. Transfer to a platter.

Heat the remaining oil in the same wok and add the ginger and garlic. Stir a few times until fragrant , then stir the beef mixture again and pour into the wok. Stir constantly for about 2 minutes, or until the beef is almost done. Return the peppers to the wok and give a few big stirs with a spatula until well mixed and heated. Taste and add salt if necessary. Serve immediately.

As a meal in its own right, this needs no accompaniment other than rice or noodles.

FAMILY-STYLE FRIED RICE

SERVES 3 – 5

450 g/1 lb cold cooked
   long-grain white rice
2 large eggs
1 teaspoon rice wine or dry
   sherry
3–4 spring onions, thinly sliced
1 teaspoon salt, or to taste
4 tablespoons vegetable oil
6 tablespoons frozen peas
50–85 g/2–3 oz ham, chopped

Place the rice in a large bowl and use your fingers to break up any lumps. Break the eggs over the rice and add the rice wine, spring onions and salt. Mix together with a wooden spoon or your hands until well blended.

Heat the oil in a wok over high heat. When the oil is hot, add the rice mixture and stir constantly for about 5 minutes, then add the peas and ham and continue stirring for another 5 minutes or until the rice is loose, fluffy and completely heated through. Taste and add more salt if desired. Serve hot.

Often served as a lunch or snack in China, fried rice goes well with grilled meat or seafood, in place of potatoes.

The Basics

Glossary of Chinese ingredients

BEAN CURD

Also known by its Japanese name of tofu, this important ingredient is highly nutritious, very low in saturated fat, and has little discernible taste of its own. Fresh bean curd is sold in cakes and comes in a variety of textures, from custardy-soft (silken) to firm. For stir-frying use Chinese-style firm bean curd. In soups you may use the softer Japanese variety.

BEAN PASTE

A thick, salty paste made of fermented soy beans. It is available either puréed or with whole beans. Japanese bean paste is called miso. Do not confuse bean paste with black bean sauce.

GINGER

An irregularly shaped, fibrous rhizome; look for a smooth, shiny, tan-coloured skin and firm, rock-hard root. Do not substitute ground ginger. An average slice is about 4 cm/1 ½ inches in diameter and 3 mm/⅛ inch thick.

GOLDEN NEEDLES

The name describes the appearance of these dried lily flowers. They must be softened before use by soaking them in hot water for about 30 minutes. They should then be rinsed, drained and squeezed to remove most of the water. Used in vegetarian and many Northern Chinese dishes.

HOISIN SAUCE

A thick, spicy-sweet sauce made of fermented soy beans, garlic, vinegar, sugar and spices. Use for cooking or as a dipping sauce.

MANDARIN PANCAKES

These fine wheat pancakes are sold fresh or frozen in Asian supermarkets. Steam to reheat. They are served as an accompaniment to Peking duck and other dishes; the idea is to spread the pancake with hoisin or plum sauce, perhaps sprinkle on some shredded spring onion or cucumber, then add the meat and use your fingers to roll up the pancake.

NOODLES

Chinese cuisine uses many varieties of noodles. In the wheat-growing north, wheat flour noodles, known as *mian*, are favoured over rice noodles. They are available fresh or dried. Follow the cooking instructions on the package, being careful not to overcook fresh noodles. In general, the Chinese prefer a texture slightly softer than al dente (the firm-to-the-bite texture recommended for Italian dishes). Noodles symbolize long life and are served long and uncut at birthday meals.

RICE WINE

Shaoxing rice wine is China's famous wine. You may substitute pale, dry sherry if you wish.

SESAME SEED OIL

Chinese sesame seed oil is an aromatic, amber-coloured oil pressed from roasted sesame seeds. It is different from the cold-pressed sesame seed oil used in some Western cooking. A low smoking temperature makes this oil unsuitable for stir-frying. It is usually sprinkled over the food just before serving, to add its distinctive flavour.

SOY SAUCE

Soy sauces from China are recommended. Light soy sauce refers to the thin texture of the sauce; it may be replaced with a Japanese soy sauce. Dark soy sauce contains molasses or caramel, which give it a darker colour, sweeter taste and thicker texture. Always look for naturally brewed soy sauce.

SZECHUAN PEPPERCORNS

Known as 'flower pepper' in Chinese, these small, reddish-brown peppercorns add a rich, aromatic flavour. When used in large amounts, they cause a slight numbing sensation to the mouth. Before use, toast by heating them in an ungreased frying pan over medium heat until fragrant. Leave to cool, then grind to a powder with a pestle and mortar.

WOOD EARS

A tree fungus, also known as cloud ears or black fungus, that is sold dried. Before use it must be softened by soaking in hot water until soft and pliable. It should then be rinsed, drained and squeezed to remove most of the water. It has very little flavour and is used primarily for its black colour and chewy texture, to contrast with other ingredients.

MENU PLANNING

A traditional Chinese meal consists of a number of main dishes with rice and a soup. In general, prepare two or three dishes plus a soup for four adults, adding a main dish for every two additional guests. For family-style meals, all the dishes are served at once. Chinese food can also be served Western-style, with one dish as a main course, accompanied by steamed rice.

Dessert is rarely served, except for banquets or special occasions. Fresh or canned fruit, such as lychees, tangerines, mangoes or a colourful fruit salad, is an excellent ending to any Chinese meal.

When planning your menu, look for variety in colour and taste, and contrast in texture and temperature.

EQUIPMENT

You don't need a lot of specialized equipment to prepare Chinese food, but having the right tools, in the best quality you can afford, will give the best results.

THE WOK

The round-bottomed wok with small metal handles is rarely used in China any more, because most people now cook on flat burners, rather than the old-fashioned wood braziers. I recommend a flat-bottomed, 30-35cm/ 12-14 inch diameter wok with a single long handle. These can be safely used on gas, electric or ceramic hobs.

The traditionalist may choose an uncoated carbon steel pan, but nonstick woks are widely available, require less oil and do not need 'seasoning' before use. Just remember not to preheat a nonstick wok when it is empty. You must add oil or some kind of liquid before heating to avoid damaging the nonstick surface.

THE KNIFE

The term 'Chinese cleaver' is a misnomer; I like to think of it as a Chinese chef's knife. It is cleaver-shaped, but its blade is thinner and lighter than the tool that is used to chop up whole chickens and large cuts of meat. The wide blade is designed to give the cook added weight for cutting everything from meat to seafood and vegetables. I like a high-carbon stainless steel blade; this will not rust, and maintains a sharp edge that is easy to resharpen on a sharpening steel.

THE STEAMER

Chinese kitchens don't have ovens, so instead of baking breads they steam them. Chinese-style steamers are multi-tiered and are made of bamboo or stainless steel.

Classic Cooking

STARTERS
Jean Christophe Novelli Chef/patron of Maison Novelli, which opened in London to great acclaim in 1996. He previously worked at the Four Seasons restaurant, London.

VEGETABLE SOUPS
Elisabeth Luard Cookery writer for the *Sunday Telegraph Magazine* and author of *European Peasant Food* and *European Festival Food*, which won a Glenfiddich Award.

GOURMET SALADS
Sonia Stevenson The first woman chef in the UK to be awarded a Michelin star, at the Horn of Plenty in Devon. Author of *The Magic of Saucery* and *Fresh Ways with Fish*.

FISH AND SHELLFISH
Gordon Ramsay Chef/proprietor of one of London's most popular restaurants, Aubergine, recently awarded its second Michelin star. He is the author of *A Passion for Flavour*.

CHICKEN, DUCK AND GAME
Nick Nairn Chef/patron of Braeval restaurant near Aberfoyle in Scotland, whose BBC-TV series *Wild Harvest* was last summer's most successful cookery series, accompanied by a book.

LIVERS, SWEETBREADS AND KIDNEYS
Simon Hopkinson Former chef/patron at London's Bibendum restaurant, columnist and author of *Roast Chicken and Other Stories* and the forthcoming *The Prawn Cocktail Years*.

VEGETARIAN
Rosamond Richardson Author of several vegetarian titles, including *The Great Green Gourmet* and *Food from Green Places*. She has also appeared on television.

PASTA
Joy Davies One of the creators of *BBC Good Food Magazine*, she has been food editor of *She, Woman* and *Options* and written for the *Guardian, Daily Telegraph* and *Harpers & Queen*.

CHEESE DISHES
Rose Elliot The UK's most successful vegetarian cookery writer and author of many books, including *Not Just a Load of Old Lentils* and *The Classic Vegetarian Cookbook*.

POTATO DISHES
Patrick McDonald Author of the forthcoming *Simply Good Food* and Harvey Nichols' food consultant.

BISTRO COOKING
Anne Willan Founder and director of La Varenne Cookery School in Burgundy and West Virginia. Author of many books and a specialist in French cuisine.

ITALIAN COOKING
Anna Del Conte is the author of *The Classic Food of Northern Italy* (chosen as the 1996 Guild of Food Writers Book of the Year) and *The Gastronomy of Italy*. She has appeared on BBC-TV's *Masterchef*.

VIETNAMESE COOKING
Nicole Routhier One of the United States' most popular cookery writers, her books include *Cooking Under Wraps, Nicole Routhier's Fruit Cookbook* and the award-winning *The Foods of Vietnam*.

MALAYSIAN COOKING
Jill Dupleix One of Australia's best known cookery writers, with columns in the *Sydney Morning Herald* and *Elle*. Author of *New Food, Allegro al dente* and the Master Chefs *Pacific*.

PEKING CUISINE
Helen Chen Learned to cook traditional Peking dishes from her mother, Joyce Chen, the grande dame of Chinese cooking in the United States. The author of *Chinese Home Cooking*.

STIR FRIES
Kay Fairfax Author of several books, including *100 Great Stir-fries, Homemade* and *The Australian Christmas Book*.

NOODLES
Terry Durack Australia's most widely read restaurant critic and co-editor of the *Sydney Morning Herald Good Food Guide*. He is the author of *YUM!*, a book of stories and recipes.

NORTH INDIAN CURRIES
Pat Chapman Started the Curry Club in 1982. Appears regularly on television and radio and is the author of eighteen books, the latest being *The Thai Restaurant Cookbook*.

BARBECUES AND GRILLS
Brian Turner Chef/patron of Turner's in Knightsbridge and one of Britain's most popular food broadcasters; he appears frequently on *Ready Steady Cook, Food and Drink* and many other television programmes.

SUMMER AND WINTER CASSEROLES
Anton Edelmann Maître Chef des Cuisines at the Savoy Hotel, London, and author of six books. He appears regularly on BBC-TV's *Masterchef*.

TRADITIONAL PUDDINGS
Tessa Bramley Chef/patron of the acclaimed Old Vicarage restaurant in Ridgeway, Derbyshire. Author of *The Instinctive Cook*, and a regular presenter on a new Channel 4 daytime series *Here's One I Made Earlier*.

DECORATED CAKES
Jane Asher Author of several cookery books and a novel. She has also appeared in her own television series, *Jane Asher's Christmas* (1995).

FAVOURITE CAKES
Mary Berry One of Britain's leading cookery writers, her numerous books include *Mary Berry's Ultimate Cake Book*. She has made many television and radio appearances and is a regular contributor to cookery magazines.

Photographs © Simon Wheeler 1997

First published in 1997 by
George Weidenfeld & Nicolson
The Orion Publishing Group
Orion House
5 Upper St Martin's Lane
London WC2H 9EA

British Library Cataloguing-in-Publication data
A catalogue record for this book is available from the
British Library

ISBN 0 297 82278 0

Designed by Lucy Holmes
Edited by Maggie Ramsay
Food styling by Joy Davies
Typeset by Tiger Typeset